The Talent Show

Schoolies™

Based on the characters created by
Ellen Crimi-Trent

priddy books

One morning, Mrs. Hedge asked the Schoolies an interesting question.

Then Chip spoke up.

Mrs. Hedge told the Schoolies that soon there would be a School Talent Show. Everyone was looking forward to it, especially Chip!

Chip practiced singing.
He sang, and sang, and sang.

Leeza loved to perform, but her sister Lydia was shy and didn't want to be in the Talent Show. So Mrs. Hedge gave Lydia a special job.

The Schoolies were very excited.

First, it was Hayden's turn
to show his talent.

Then, Leeza performed the part of a princess.

Spencer did a roller skating trick.

Then C.J. Crawley painted a picture, while Kitty played piano. Backstage, Chip started to feel nervous.

Soon, it was time for Chip to sing.
He went out onto the stage.

It was very quiet.

Chip nodded.
Lydia took a deep breath,
then she walked on stage
and held Chip's hand.

Together, they began to sing.

Soon all the Schoolies were singing together. Everybody in the audience clapped.

At the end of the show, Chip and Lydia took a bow together.